KNOWING YOUR IDENTITY IN CHRIST

JENNIFER L. TORO

Knowing Your Identity in Christ

Trilogy Christian Publishers, a Wholly Owned Subsidary of the Trinity Broadcasting Network

2442 Michelle Drive, Tustin, CA 92780

Rights Department, 2442 Michelle Drive, Tustin, CA 92780.

Trilogy Christian Publishing/TBN and colophon are trademarks of Trinity Broadcasting Network.

For information about special discounts for bulk purchases, please contact Trilogy Christian Publishing.

Trilogy Disclaimer: The views and content expressed in this book are those of the author and may not necessarily reflect the views and doctrine of Trilogy Christian Publishing or the Trinity Broadcasting Network.

Manufactured in the United States of America

10 9 8 7 6 5 4 3 2 1

Library of Congress Cataloging-in-Publication Data is available.

ISBN: 978-1-63769-866-2

E-ISBN: 978-1-63769-867-9

DEDICATION

This book is first dedicated to the Father, the Son, and the Holy Spirit, who continue to love and strengthen me.

~

To my loving family, whose loving arms are always open.

~

ACKNOWLEDGMENTS

Thank You, Jesus, for saving me and giving me a second chance in life. You've transformed me into a person I never thought I could be—full of love, joy, and peace. You are my Rock, and my Fortress, and the love of my life.

This book would not at all be possible without You; You are the head of this book and the real author.

Thank You.

To my wonderful family, who loves me regardless of my flaws. Thank you for loving me unconditionally, and I hope you can find comfort and joy in this book.

I love you all very much!

TBN and Trilogy, thank you for this amazing opportunity to share the message God has placed on my heart. TBN has been a blessing to me throughout the years, and it's an honor to be a part of the Trilogy family.

May God continue to bless you all exceedingly abundantly above all that you can ask, think, or imagine, as you continue to expand the kingdom of God on the earth.

TABLE OF CONTENTS

INTRODUCTION

God has openly made available to us salvation, for-giveness, authority, power, armor, His Holy Spirit, and so much more. People may be aware of these things but are not sure how to apply them to their lives. May this book be a guide to help you live up to the amazing standard God has set for your life. A life of freedom, sonship, authority, and hope.

God did not leave us orphans; He sent us His Holy Spirit, who would give us remembrance of the words that Jesus spoke here on the earth and that He is still speaking to us. Jesus said in John 16:13 (NKJV), *"However, when He, the Spirit of truth, has come, He will guide you into all truth; for He will not speak on His own authority, but whatever He hears He will speak; and He will tell you things to come."* The Holy Spirit speaks throughout the Bible, even after the death and resurrection of Jesus. He also speaks to us in our prayer time and in our everyday life. It is amazing to hear the words of Jesus, but hearing and living them are two different things. Yes, the Word of God is for you!

Sometimes the Bible scriptures are read over, but not grasped or delved into so that they're understood. When studying the Word, we must take the scriptures and root them in our heart, mind, and soul, meaning we must believe in them. In order to keep standing in this fight daily, it is vital that we have the Word of God as our foundation, that we believe the scriptures no matter what we see or experience in the physical realm. Remember, the spiritual realm existed before the physical one; the physical world came from the spiritual. God's Word is the final authority in heaven and earth. Like on earth, we have laws—for example, you stop at a red light and you go at a green one; you don't steal or break any laws because there are penalties for doing so. Breaking the law means something is done that's illegal. It's the same thing in the spirit realm; there is illegal activity done against the believer, and guess what—we have the rule book and must exercise our authority and proclaim the written Word and arrest the oppressor, the adversary!

Satan comes to kill, steal, and destroy, and these are considered illegal activities according to God's Word. The enemy comes to oppress—to bring anxiety, division, and a ton of other things to destroy our joy, peace, and loving heart toward one another and even our heart toward God. There are Christians whom the enemy has handicapped and as a result do not live to the full potential of God's best. *But Jesus.*

Jesus has done it all for us at the cross of Calvary. As born-again believers, we have the right to walk in authority, with our heads held high, and knowing that we are filled with the power of the Holy Ghost. We sit in heavenly places with Christ Jesus, and we are joint heirs with Christ.

Let's take a look at those verses:

> *But God, who is rich in mercy, because of His great love with which He loved us, even when we were dead in trespasses, made us alive together with Christ (by grace you have been saved), and raised us up together, and made us sit together in heavenly places in Christ Jesus, that in the ages to come He might show the exceeding riches of His grace in His kindness toward us in Christ Jesus.*

Ephesians 2:4-7 (NKJV)

> *The Spirit Himself bears witness with our spirit that we are children of God, and if children, then heirs—heirs of God and joint heirs with Christ, if indeed we suffer with Him, that we may also be glorified together.*

Romans 8:16-17 (NKJV)

We are one with Jesus, and His Holy Spirit lives inside of us. The enemy can't do whatever he wants with us because we are the property of heaven. The enemy has to check with God before he does anything to attack us. Let us look at the story of Job. We see in Job 1:10 that Satan acknowledged that God had placed a hedge of protection around Job and his possessions. He knew he couldn't touch Job unless God gave him permission. I am sure he went and checked out Job way before this conversation with God and thought, *There is no way I can touch him.* My brothers and sisters, that hedge of protection is around you and me. *"The Lord is my light and my salvation; whom shall I fear? The Lord is the strength of my life; of whom shall I be afraid?"* (Psalm 27:1-2 NKJV). Even though we saw all the terrible things Job confronted—from the death of his children to being covered from head to toe in sores—he retained his faith in God.

There is no need to walk in fear as a believer in Christ. When the adversary comes around and tries with all his might to knock us down like he did Job, remember, he has limits that he cannot cross. I remember one day the Lord gave me a vision of the beach. I saw the water come onto the seashore and how it receded back. The Lord spoke to me and said, "The same way I've set limits as to how far this water can come in, the same way the adversary has limits as to what he can do."

Now I want you to stop and think about what areas in your life you may be feeling attacked in, or if you have questions like: "Why is this happening to me?" Remember, when Satan went before God's throne, it was not Satan who first mentioned Job, it was God. See, God knew Job's heart and where it stood with Him. Job was considered because God knew He would be able to overcome; He knew that at the end, Job would not abandon has faith. Job said, "Naked came I out of my mother's womb, and naked will I return!" He held on to nothing of this world and understood that everything he had acquired was from the Lord, and if it all was taken away, he was fine with that. Maybe that's your case; maybe you've been considered to go through a fiery trial that God knows you'll be able to overcome, because He designed you that way. It doesn't mean you won't face frustration or question God, but you'll hold on till the end.

CHAPTER 1

Strategies and Territories

The spiritual realm consists of territories and strategies of the enemy. We have good territories like church, neutral territories like the mall, and dark territories like clubs and bars. Like in the book of Job, we are hedged all around us under the protection of Jesus Christ. His blood marks us, and we are separated from the world. Now the enemy's tactics are to try and take us out of that protection through our freewill decisions.

Let us look at the Prodigal Son in the book of Luke 15:11-32. The son had everything in the father's house, yet he chose to take his inheritance and travel to a distant country, where he lived a wild life. After he had spent all that he had, a great famine came upon the land, and he was left with nothing to eat. The Bible says he then joined himself to a citizen of that country, who sent him to feed his swine. Now in the Old Testament scriptures, swine are considered unclean; you are not to touch or eat them, so you can only imagine the rock bottom he had hit. He went out into the fields to feed them and desired the food they were eating. Eventually, he came to himself and made the journey back to his father's house, where he was greeted by his overjoyed father and a grand feast was made in his honor.

We always see the story of the Prodigal Son through the eyes of the forgiving father, which is fine, but let us look through the lens of the son. What must have drawn him out of the father's house, where he had everything and anything he could have imagined? I am sure his father would have done anything for him and seeing that he gave his son the inheritance without resistance speaks volumes about his character. See, God does not beg us to stay if we choose to leave. He honors our freewill, even if we're not making the best decisions. God will warn us through people and dreams, but the decision is ultimately ours to serve Him or not.

The Prodigal Son was drawn out of the house by the deceitfulness of sin. The enemy will always try to make us feel as if we're missing out on what the world has to offer. He parades himself through entertainment, music, the glitz and glam of the fashion world, and so on, which Christians who are in those types of industries can tell you do not fill the void—only Jesus can. He makes a false narrative that the grass is greener on the other side, but it's an attempt to lure us away from the safety of the covering of Christ and to then try to wreak havoc in our lives.

Now if he can't lure us out of the hedge of protection, he will try to get us to crack open a door or a window. For example, your past will come up. It could be an old flame, an old friend, or an old coworker who knew who you were before coming to Christ. These people will be tools in the hand of the enemy to try to get you to walk backward instead of forward, making you think it's okay to dwell on the past. Remember, 2 Corinthians 5:17 (NKJV) says, *"Therefore, if anyone is in Christ, he is a new creation; old things have passed away; behold, all things have become new."*

I remember a friend of mine who had gotten baptized a year after I did. I told her, "You watch: your ex is going to come back, because it happened to me." A few days later he sure did, and she was baffled. He called her and said, "I was thinking about you and decided to give you a call." She told me she hadn't spoken to him in years, and that it was odd that he called. Something similar happened to me after getting baptized. One of my family members bumped into my first boyfriend soon after I started serving the Lord. We ended up speaking for a few weeks, and then I soon realized it was not God's will and ended the connection immediately. We must be careful of the enemy's traps and have our spiritual eyes open to discern what's from God and what's not from God. Not everyone from the past is bad, because you can minister to them and they can see the transformation God has done in you, but if they don't want to hear about God or church then be careful, because they can be used as a tool to take you off course.

GUARD YOUR HEART

The heart is an interesting place—it holds our thoughts and sentiments and is extremely fragile. It should be handled with extreme care. A poisoned heart is a dangerous thing for oneself and others around them. It'll cause a person to live a life that's less than God's best. The Bible says in Proverbs 4:23 (NKJV), *"Keep your heart with all diligence, for out of it spring the issues of life."* The Complete Jewish Bible states, *"Above everything else, guard your heart; for it is the source of life's consequences."* Guarding our hearts from hurt, unforgiveness, bitterness, jealousy, envy, and revenge is vital, because it'll set the course of our lives. We are not exempt from ever feeling these emotions; we will, but we should be careful we don't let them permeate and grow roots in our hearts.

In Genesis 25, Esau, Isaac's oldest son, came home one day weary from the field. He was exhausted and starving, and Jacob, his twin brother, happened to be cooking some stew. Out of Esau's desperation, he begged Jacob for some of the stew, but it wasn't without a price. Jacob asked Esau for his birthright, and Esau without hesitation gave it away. The birthright was a double portion of the property the firstborn received when the father died. Esau gave up his double portion of blessing, and when he tried to receive it from Isaac, his father, before Isaac's death, he couldn't, even though he cried hysterically. God calls this type of person profane. In Hebrews 12:14-17 (NKJV), it says, *"Pursue peace with all people, and holiness, without which no one will see the Lord: looking carefully lest anyone fall short of the grace of God; lest any root of bitterness springing up cause trouble, and by this many become defiled; lest there be any fornicator or profane person like Esau, who for one morsel of food sold his birthright. For you know that afterward, when he wanted to inherit the blessing, he was rejected, for he found no place for repentance, though he sought it diligently with tears."* Esau represents someone who would throw away their inheritance in Jesus Christ for a morsel of bitterness, envy, or strife. Our eternal salvation is at stake if these emotions become rooted in our hearts, but we can always go to Jesus, confess it, and ask to be forgiven and healed. He will more than gladly come to our succor and put His balm on our hearts and make things right again.

PRAYER

Prayer is an intimate communication with the Lord. You can tell Him whatever's on your heart. It's a place of expression and a judgment-free zone. Sometimes people say, "How can I tell this to a holy God—how will He view me?" When I go into prayer, sometimes I imagine God, high and lifted up on His throne yet leaning in, listening with compassion to my prayers. The Bible says in Psalm

138:6 (NKJV), *"Though the Lord is on high, yet He regards the lowly; but the proud He knows from afar."* When we open up to Him in prayer, we are acknowledging who He is: our Father. What you say will never change His view of you or the fact that you are His child. I encourage you to open your heart and leave any reservations behind.

Prayer is also a place where we can release spiritual toxins. When we bottle up hurt, disappointment, anger, guilt, and insecurity, we're like a soda bottle being shaken up—compressed inside where if the wrong person turns the top, they'll receive an eruption of unhealthy emotion that wasn't merited. When we release those toxins to Jesus, He takes the burden off, and we give Him the ability to work in us and heal our wounds. See, God already knows what's going on deep down inside of us—sometimes things we don't even know we carry. But the things we do know, He wants us to confess to Him—that is key—and then He will bring out the rest. Communication is important in any relationship, and believe me, God is all ears when we pray. Hebrews 4:13 (NKJV) says, *"And there is no creature hidden from His sight, but all things are naked and open to the eyes of Him to whom we must give account."* Let us be honest about things He already knows and feel safe enough to be open in His presence.

FAITH

Expect your faith to be tested in this walk. Faith is what connects us to an unseen God. If our faith is broken, then what can we hang on to? Faith is like what a network is to a cellphone. Without the network, we'll be dialing a number and hearing nothing on the other line. Hebrews 11:6 (NKJV) says, *"But without faith it is impossible to please Him, for he who comes to God must believe that He is, and that He is a rewarder of those who diligently seek Him."* People received their miracles in the Bible because they believed Jesus could do it.

Now one thing the enemy loves to jump on is when things don't go our way—another setback happens, or you prayed for a sick person who didn't get well. Regardless of the situation, we must have this fact rooted down in us: that God is still in full control. Never blame yourself, thinking that something didn't work out because you didn't have enough faith. At the end, God has His perfect will. Isaiah 55:8-9 (NKJV) says, *" 'For My thoughts are not your thoughts, nor are your ways My ways,' says the Lord. 'For as the heavens are higher than the earth, so are My ways higher than your ways, and My thoughts than your thoughts.' "* Some circumstances we'll never fully understand, but the greatest truth we can hold on to is that we don't go through anything alone. So, when things seem haywire—a door closes, your life takes an unexpected turn, or God seems silent—know that God is still on the throne, and He is working in your favor. Life may not come together like you've thought—you might not be married yet or have that great paying career you've always dreamed of—but don't lose faith just because you don't see it happening right now. God takes His time, but at the end, it's worth the wait. And remember, we have a faithful Friend named the Holy Spirit to confide in and lift us up through anything.

In Ephesians 6:16, Paul compares faith to a shield. Faith is what is going to cover you through the ebbs and flows of life. No matter what you hear about whatever circumstance, you can be assured that God's got it. Now this is not to minimize painful situations like death, sickness, betrayals, or losing a job. There are situations that genuinely hurt and leave us questioning the Lord as to why, but I want to position you in a way that you will always fall back on your faith when life tries to knock you down. Never stray from what you know is true about God: that He is good. Hold on to your faith, regardless of what has come your way, and know that God will bring you through to the other side.

PEACE

Jesus says in John 14:27 (KJV), *"Peace I leave with you, my peace I give unto you: not as the world giveth, give I unto you. Let not your heart be troubled, neither let it be afraid."* Peace is one of the fruits of the Holy Spirit, and guess what—if you've accepted Jesus Christ as your Lord and Savior, that same Spirit lives inside of you. Peace is given freely to us by God, but it's still something we have to guard. Our thoughts are the focal point of our peace. We can lose our peace if we meditate on the wrong things, like fear, worry, a mistake at work, or the news broadcasts. Yes, we are going to confront situations that are unpleasant, like being treated unfairly or being talked about in a negative light, but how many of those situations are you going to let affect you? What is worth you losing your peace? Don't give it away so easily; guard it, and don't give the wrong people power over you.

The realm of the mind is where the battle is; we have to take our thoughts into captivity if they don't align with what God has spoken over us. We need to guard our thought life. Paul says in Philippians 4:8-9 (NKJV), *"Finally, brethren, whatever things are true, whatever things are noble, whatever things are just, whatever things are pure, whatever things are lovely, whatever things are of good report, if there is any virtue and if there is anything praiseworthy—meditate on these things. The things which you learned and received and heard and saw in me, these do, and the God of peace will be with you."* If you are a person who suffers from anxiety or panic attacks, I want you to pinpoint where it starts. What thoughts provoke you to be fearful? And I want you to search the Bible and find what verse or verses would counter that thought. Then I want you to speak that Word until you believe it's true and it destroys what is trying to bring you down. This is a war, and we have the Sword which is the Word of God, and it can take down the biggest giants in the spirit realm.

God has equipped us with His Holy Spirit; His Word and His blood cover us. I can remember a time when I was on a crowded train in New York City. Rush hour was at its climax, and I was sitting in the corner next to the door that leads you to the next cart. All of a sudden, I felt anxiety and anxious thoughts that said, "Who am I and where am I?" I had never had thoughts like that, ever, and I felt panic. I closed my eyes and said, "The blood of Jesus covers me," and in a split second, it was gone. A lot of people think that all thoughts are their thoughts, because they come in the first person, but that is not always the case. They are deceptive spirits, and we must learn to identify them and plead the blood of Jesus, or exercise authority over them in the name of Jesus, and they have to flee.

SALVATION

Salvation is the greatest gift given to the world through Jesus Christ. We get a clean slate when we acknowledge our sins to Him and accept Him as our Lord and Savior. We have a chance to start anew. 1 John 1:9 (NKJV) says, *"If we confess our sins, He is faithful and just to forgive us our sins and to cleanse us from all unrighteousness."* We are transferred from the kingdom of darkness to the kingdom of Jesus Christ! How exciting! After we receive this precious salvation, it needs to be maintained, treasured, and protected. It's like the man in Matthew 13:45-46 who sold all that he had, to buy the pearl of great price. He let everything go for that precious pearl, and we ought to do the same. Let me explain: Jesus said in Matthew 10:39 (NKJV), *"He who finds his life will lose it, and he who loses his life for My sake will find it."* Finding one's life outside of Christ will cause a person to lose their eternal salvation. So, they can have everything they may want in life—success, a career—but someone just living a comfortable life will ultimately pay the price in the afterlife of eternal separation from God, because they never made the decision to give their lives to Jesus. It doesn't matter if these people are good or bad; our eternity depends on that one decision. To lose one's life means to give up your life of sin to serve Jesus on the earth, and then you'll have eternal life at the end. Is it a struggle? Yes, but it's worth it to serve Jesus.

Now salvation is not easily lost. We are being refined day by day. There are going to be bumps and bruises along the way, but God continues His work in us if we allow Him to. After we receive Christ as our Lord and Savior, Paul says in Ephesians 1:13-14 (NKJV), *"In Him you also trusted, after you heard the word of truth, the gospel of your salvation; in whom also, having believed, you were sealed with the Holy Spirit of promise, who is the guarantee of our inheritance until the redemption of the purchased possession, to the praise of His glory."* I like to think of the Holy Spirit as an engagement ring. The engagement ring represents a promise from a man to a woman meaning soon, they'll marry. We have the Holy Spirit as the promise from the Father that Jesus will come back for us. In the meantime, the Holy Spirit leads us into the truth of God's Word and chips off whatever's not Christlike. It's definitely a molding process.

Some Christians believe that they've lost their salvation because they made a mistake and sinned. They think that God runs away and wants nothing do with them, but it's the complete opposite. Remember when Adam and Eve sinned, and God came looking for them in the garden? He knew what had happened, but He called out for Adam anyway. It's the sin itself that makes us feel far from the Lord. Like when Jesus was on the cross, taking the weight of the world's sin on Himself, He yelled out in Matthew 27:46 (NKJV), *"My God, My God, why have You forsaken Me?"* Even the Son of God felt the separation from God that sin causes.

Now I'm not one of those who believes in "once saved, always saved." The Bible never speaks of anything like it. The only way a person can lose their salvation is by continually resisting the correction from the Lord and choosing to sin; eventually, the Holy Spirit departs. When a person no longer feels the conviction of the Holy Spirit and continues to sin without caring, they are in a major danger zone. 1 Timothy 4:1-2 speaks of people who have their conscience seared with a hot iron, meaning they suppressed the good they knew they should be doing. Look what happened to Israel in the desert after they made the golden calf while Moses was on the mountain with God and the Ten Commandments: Exodus 32:31-33 (NKJV), *"Then Moses returned to the Lord and said, 'Oh, these people have committed a great sin, and have made for themselves a god of gold! Yet now, if You will forgive their sin—but if not, I pray, blot me out of Your book which You have written.' And the Lord said to Moses, 'Whoever has sinned against Me, I will blot him out of My book.'"* The people had no conviction in their actions and had abandoned God completely. Then it says in the book of Revelation 22:18-19 (NKJV), *"For I testify to everyone who hears the words of the prophecy of this book: If anyone adds to these things, God will add to him the plagues that are written in this book; and if anyone takes away from the words of the book of this prophecy, God shall take away his part from the Book of Life, from the holy city, and from the things which are written in this book."* What Israel did to God in the wilderness: Isaiah 63:9-10 (KJV), *"In all their affliction he was afflicted, and the angel of his presence saved them: in his love and in his pity he redeemed them; and he bare them, and carried them all the days of old. But they rebelled, and vexed his Holy Spirit: therefore he was turned to be their enemy, and he fought against them.* " And here is what Paul says about someone who does not have the Holy Spirit, in Romans 8:9 (NKJV), *"But you are not in the flesh but in the Spirit, if indeed the Spirit of God dwells in you. Now if anyone does not have the Spirit of Christ, he is not His. "*

We are all going to slip and fall, but the key is not to make it a habit and abuse the grace of God. Whatever your weakness is, present it to the Lord and be honest with Him. He'll strengthen you through the power of His Holy Spirit to overcome temptation. No matter how hard it is to say no to your weakness, you always have a choice; yield to the Holy Spirit, and when you submit to God, the devil has to flee from you! The more you submit to God, the more you'll notice yourself getting stronger in the Spirit, because you are crucifying the flesh. You're saying no to yourself and yes to God, and what used to make you stumble won't have power over you anymore.

> *No temptation has overtaken you except such as is common to man; but God is faithful, who will not allow you to be tempted beyond what you are able, but with the temptation will also make the way of escape, that you may be able to bear it.*

1 Corinthians 10:13 (NKJV)

Therefore submit to God. Resist the devil and he will flee from you.

James 4:7 (NKJV)

CHAPTER 2

Expand Your Territory

We are designed to grow and evolve in our walk with
Christ. He is ever working on us so that we can become
more like Him. Our bad tempters, unhealthy habits, and
earthly way of thinking slowly start to change as we continually leave the door open for Jesus to transform us. He'll
take us to new levels of glory. What used to make you tick,
you can now brush it off; if someone bumps you on the
subway, you're a little nicer in how you respond. These
are all little victories to celebrate! It's a sign that the Holy
Spirit is working in you.

Now in order for God to take you to another level, it
entails you passing tests. When you hear someone talking
about you at the office, at school, or even at church, the test
is, how will you respond? Will you make a big deal about
it and lose your cool, or leave it alone? This can really go
many ways, but dealing with these issues in a Christlike
way is what will really make you shine. I can remember a
time when I was hired to work in a hospital, and the woman who helped me get the job turned on me and didn't like
some of my life views. I noticed that certain people stopped
talking to me, and she was saying things about me that I

honestly can't remember. So, I started talking to Jesus in the break room, and He said to me, "What I think about you is what matters." That truly took the weight of worry off of me and put a smile on my face—to this day, those words are with me, and I don't let anyone get me down. I was eventually moved from the office I shared with this person to another area, and it was like coming into a whole new world, where people favored me. This person who had tried to make my life impossible was not viewed in a positive light by others in the office, and I was told, "We have your back." What God thinks about you will surpass someone's negative view of you and position you in a place where people will favor you.

The process is not always easy; there are times when you may feel you're holding on for dear life. I say this because we'll always have a struggle with our old man, the human nature that's contrary to God. You can read about it in Galatians 5:16-26—it's the age-old war between the flesh and the Spirit. "Eye for an eye, tooth for a tooth," the flesh yells, but the Holy Spirit now says, "Love your enemies, bless those who curse you, and do good to those who hate you." This is definitely not something we can do on our own; the Holy Spirit helps us in the transition to love. Going back to my experience at the hospital: yes, there were times when I wanted to respond and defend myself, and I did once, but I had to think—was it really worth losing my job? Sometimes you'll deal with people who are truly not sorry for their actions against you, and you have to leave them in God's hands. Remember, the fight is not between flesh and blood, and sometimes not responding to an attack is the most powerful weapon you can use.

KING DAVID

King David was a man of war who killed many of the Lord's enemies. We know him to have had repeated wars with the Philistines and as the one who killed Goliath. I want us to go back to a period in David's life where he was heavily persecuted by King Saul. David hadn't done anything deserving of being treated this way. David was faithful to Israel and King Saul, but Saul became jealous of David when the people praised David more for killing Goliath. This sent Saul down a path of wanting to destroy David.

David remained faithful while Saul persecuted him; he didn't fight back but would literally run for his life. He had chances to kill Saul, like in the cave in 1 Samuel 24, when Saul came in to relieve himself and David and his men were in the sides of the cave. David's men told him the Lord was delivering Saul into his hands, but instead David cut the skirt of Saul's robe and his heart smote him. Whenever it's in your hand to do your enemy harm, don't take the offer, because it'll make you just like them. We have to take the higher way in instances like this, or else we'll be found guilty—and God does not play favorites.

Now imagine if David had taken advantage of the opportunity and had killed Saul. I truly believe David's kingdom would not have been established. David always knew that God would deal with Saul. In the natural, anyone would look at the scene and say, "This is it! The ultimate revenge for everything Saul has put David through," but there is a verse in Proverbs 14:12 (NKJV) that says, *"There is a way that seems right to a man, but its end is the way of death."* Sometimes following what's right doesn't make sense in the natural realm, and acting out of compulsion can hinder what destiny God has planned for us. God is not looking for our comfort; He is looking for our obedience.

Saul eventually died in battle, like David suspected he would. David passed the test. After intense struggles and running for his life, he made it to the end of the fiery trial in victory. God will take care of your enemies; we don't wish people evil, but the battle is the Lord's, and those who resist Him will pay a price. After Saul's death it seemed like the windows of heaven opened for David. God established him as king of Israel and then Judah, and he started to expand his territory. He won battle after battle; he conquered Jerusalem and named the stronghold there the City of David; the Philistines came up after they heard David was anointed king, and they were defeated. Here are some other nations that King David subdued and made servants of: Moab, Ammon, Amalek, the Philistines, Edom, and Syria, and he recovered territory at the River Euphrates after defeating Hadadezer the son of king Zobah. After David pushed through and overcame, the promises of God started to manifest themselves, and David saw the glory of God over and over again. What battle may you be facing currently, where you feel you can't hold on? I encourage you to stay in the fight like David did and let God be your refuge and strength. Never take matters into your own hands but always yield to the Lord, even when it doesn't make sense. The Bible says in Romans 8:28 (NKJV), *"And we know that all things work together for good to those who love God, to those who are the called according to His purpose."* God will turn it around for your good, even though you really can't see it now. Trust that He will get you through whatever you're confronting.

Imagine what is waiting for you on the other side of your obedience in the trial: a pastoral ministry? A teaching position? A husband or wife? A career, a business? The trials we go through are specifically designed by God to form us for the calling. Nothing enters your life without God knowing it and without His permission. Trials are not meant to destroy you—they are meant to form you. Now the key is to stay in God's will during the trial; if not, it could be a different outcome that's not in your favor.

David's victory over the trial approved him to be king of Israel. David, you could say, was bent, bruised, crushed, betrayed—and at the end, faultless before the Lord. Sometimes the enemy will try to break us, but hold on, and you will see the glory of God in your life the way King David did.

Your enemies are who God uses to propel you into your destiny. When Jesus was being crucified, they thought they were doing away with Him. Little did they know that they were pushing Him to the next level of glory, promoting Him to the right hand of the Father. You can't expand your territory if there is no resistance. Here is what the Livestrong website has to say about what happens to our muscles when we work out. Muscle changes start with resistance exercises. Whether you're going for a run, doing pushups, or lifting barbells, resistance is being placed on your muscles. When the resistance is greater than what your body typically encounters during the day through your regular routine, the process of muscle *hypertrophy*, or muscle building, is activated. Now when we don't exercise our muscles, something happens called muscle *atrophy*, which is a decrease in muscle mass. When there is no resistance, we become weak. If our faith is not challenged, it will not grow. If there weren't any problems, would we really pray as much? Romans 5:3-4 (NKJV) says, *"And not only that, but we also glory in tribulations, knowing that tribulation produces perseverance; and perseverance, character; and character, hope. "* When tribulations come, let us see it as another opportunity to get to the next level that God has ordained for us.

MAINTENANCE

It's always good to stop and rest for a while, whether it be at work, taking care of the kids, or driving. As long as we go "express" 24/7, we'll be subject to something called burnout. There's nothing wrong with having a busy schedule, appointments, and meetings, but it's most important to take care of ourselves and not stretch ourselves too thin. God cares about our mental, spiritual, and physical well-being. He crafted us in love and care and doesn't want us running around jaded.

A car needs maintenance about every six months where the tires are rotated, the oil is changed if necessary, the brakes are checked, and so on; likewise, we need maintenance before the Father. David said in Psalm 63:1 (NKJV), *"O God, You are my God; early will I seek You; my soul thirsts for You; my flesh longs for You in a dry and thirsty land where there is no water. "* These moments, I believe, happen to every believer, no matter how long you've served the Lord. We'll encounter these times of desperation and thirst for the Spirit of God. We always need to go to Jesus and get filled again; He's the fountain of living waters.

People have made the mistake of running on empty—running on what they "know" in ministry and not stopping and getting into the presence of the Lord to get refreshed. Jesus Himself, being the Son of God and God Himself, spent time alone with the Father on Mount Olivet and prayed all night. God always leads by example. In Genesis 2:2-3 (NKJV), God demonstrates to us what rest is: *"And on the seventh day God ended His work which He had done, and He rested on the seventh day from all His work which He had done. Then God blessed the seventh day and sanctified it, because in it He rested from all His work which God had created and made."*

Now I want to clarify that God was not tired on the seventh day and in need of sleep. According to Isaiah 40:28, He neither faints nor is weary. One of the definitions of rest in the Merriam-Webster Dictionary is "to cease from action or motion: refrain from labor or exertion." He completed creation and then ceased from His work. Sometimes it's necessary to cease from all the running around and bask in the presence of God or take a nice vacation. There, let Him give you new armor, a fresh touch of the Holy Spirit, and new strength. You'll get some joy too, since in His presence is fullness of joy (Psalm 16:11). Not only do we enjoy these blessings of being in God's presence, but the sheer fact that we get to spend time with Him is an honor in itself.

When you cease from works, please don't feel guilty.

God is pleased when you follow His lead. I'm sure some-one else can preach or give the Bible class; don't sacrifice your sanity or health if you are at your breaking point. One reason some people feel the need to overwork is because they get their validation from it. They might think, *If I'm not on the go all the time, then God will be upset with me or not love me,* and I want to say: no, that's a *big lie*! You are loved and accepted by God because you are simply His child. Yes, there are works for us to do, but everything in moderation.

CHAPTER 3

No Need to Compare

You are made in the image and likeness of God. Everything about you was specifically put in place: your hair, nose, eyes, ears, legs, voice, and so on. Comparison is the number one way to diminish how special God has made you. You have gifts, talents, and insight that no one else can deliver but you. We live in a culture where social media is prevalent—pictures are constantly uploaded of excursions, new outfits, and celebratory moments. It's a place where life can be shared with family, friends, or fans who want to follow and feel connected to your life. Even though this sounds nice—and it is—there is an unpleasant side to social media where comparison runs rampant, leaving people feeling they are not able to "measure up."

God didn't design us to covet what others have or look like, but to enjoy one another's differences and expertise. We were made like puzzle pieces; we are meant to mesh. So, where your need is, someone else can come along and assist you in that area. Hear the puzzle pieces coming together: for example, a sick person needs a doctor—*click*; your car breaks down and you need a mechanic—*click*; hungry people go to a restaurant with an excellent chef—

click; someone at church has an amazing, anointed voice that calms your seas—*click*.

Don't spend so much time worrying about what others are doing, because most likely it'll be different than what's happening in your life. Take time in the presence of God and find out who you are and what gifts He's placed inside of you. Then, when you've discovered what they are, build upon them and see how you can bless the body of Christ. Your gifts and obedience will help to edify people in a way that you will never truly know. When your heart is inclined to the Lord, He will bring things out of you that you never knew were there. There are ministries and callings that are awaiting, but we will never know what they are if we're sitting on the sidelines, watching everyone else go by, wishing we had what they did.

> *And whatever you do in word or deed, do all in the name of the Lord Jesus, giving thanks to God the Father through Him.*

Colossians 3:17 (NKJV)

STAY IN YOUR LANE

Absalom, the third-born son of King David, eyed his father's throne. He went amongst the people and treated them with extreme kindness—to the point that the Bible says he stole the hearts of the men of Israel. He conjured a rebellion against King David that dispersed David, his household, and many of his faithful servants into the wilderness. Absalom's heart was so unrepentant that he wouldn't have cared if his father had perished.

Earlier in the story, in 2 Samuel 13, the Bible mentions Absalom having a beautiful sister named Tamar. They both had an older half-brother named Amnon who was King David's firstborn. Amnon loved Tamar so much, he was lovesick; he lost weight, and Jonadab, his uncle, took notice. Jonadab was a subtle man and conjured up a plan for how Amnon could get Tamar alone. Unfortunately, the plan worked, and Amnon forced Tamar and raped her. She was humiliated and then sent away in the rudest fashion. She went to her brother Absalom's house where she was desolate. King David received the news and was angry, but didn't penalize Amnon. Absalom kept these things in his heart and two years later killed Amnon, then after a few more years tried to take his father's throne.

Absalom's conspiracy against his father comes from God's judgment on the house of David; this story can be read in 2 Samuel 11-12. Even though this betrayal was supposed to happen, it doesn't excuse the person doing the wrong. Absalom ultimately paid with his life for defying his father's kingship. The point I am trying to make with this story is to stay in your lane. Never become envious or jealous of another person's position. We all see what happened to Satan when he thought he could take on God Himself—he was cast down to the earth and judged for all eternity. Support your leaders and pray for them, even when they miss the mark. I am not excusing bad behavior, but David left us an example with the way he reverenced Saul, even though he knew he had been anointed as the next king. God has you where you are for a reason; you'll get to the position God has ordained for you in time—and of course, with your obedience. Celebrate others when you see God bless and promote them, even if they get something similar to what you've been praying for. What is reserved for you is being kept in the Father's hands—your time will come; hold on and remain faithful.

CHAPTER 4

Failure

Adam and Eve. I think most of us have blamed Adam and Eve for a lot of our hardships. I would sometimes say, "If only Eve hadn't listened to the serpent, I wouldn't be going through this! We could've been living in paradise together with God, with absolutely no problems!" Then the Lord showed me that we are all Adam and Eve, in the sense that we all have eaten the forbidden fruit. We've all sinned somewhere in our lives, and if it wasn't them, it would have been someone else—Cain and Abel being a prime example.

Adam and Eve sinned in the garden and disobeyed God, but He didn't discard them and say, "I'll make me another male and female who will obey My commands." Instead, He worked with them. In Genesis 3, after God cursed the serpent and declared to Adam and Eve the suffering they would endure, He clothed them in coats of skins. This is the first sacrifice for the atonement of sins for Adam and Eve: an animal had to die for the skins to have been produced. This shows us how quickly God wants to forgive us. God did not walk away and think about it overnight; He immediately made them animal skins and sent them off. Have you been beating yourself up over unchecked sin in your life, or do you feel no longer good enough because of mistakes you've made? Well, I've got news for you: God is not finished with you, and when we think things are over, that's where God begins.

Adam and Eve were banished from paradise, but God's command to be fruitful and multiply was still in order. Depending on the decisions we make, the plans for our lives can change, but they'll still be God's plans—He always has a plan B. The fall of Adam and Eve, and our fall, were no surprise to God. See, God is always a step ahead of you and me; there was a plan already put in place to save humanity. Jesus Christ is described in Revelation 13:8 and 1 Peter 1:20 as being the foreordained Lamb that was slain before the foundation of the world. Know that you are redeemable, even if you've messed up badly; remember, God is a creator and an artist and can craft you into someone new and give you a new purpose. He did it with the earth, in the beginning when it was without form and void; how much more us, who are made in His image and likeness?

YOU ARE NOT YOUR MISTAKES

Moses, David, and the apostle Paul are some of the greatest men in the Bible, besides Jesus, whom God used to bring about His purposes on the earth. Moses liberated Israel from Egypt, and an unforgettable miracle was the parting of the Red Sea; David took down Goliath and became a great king skilled in battle; and the apostle Paul tirelessly preached the gospel and wrote most of the New Testament books. What these men have accomplished through the power of God has echoed throughout many generations. They are testaments as to what God can do if we let Him take full control. These men, although mighty in the Bible, did not have the best history or make the best decisions while in relationship with God.

Let me list them for you:

- Moses: Killed an Egyptian.

- David: Committed adultery with Bathsheba and then had her husband Uriah killed in battle to cover her pregnancy.

- Paul: Formerly Saul, persecuted the Christian church.

Although these men had failures, they weren't defined by them. Today, when we hear their names, the great things God did through them come to mind. Your past mistakes don't have to define who you are. Jesus Christ has cleansed you with His precious blood, and it's strong enough to break the stigma off of your life. People may try to bring up your past and what you used to do, but your sins are in the sea of forgetfulness—and if Jesus isn't bringing them up, then you don't have to worry. Hold your head up and know that yesterday is in the past, never to return. You can march forward in the newness of life that has been given to you through Jesus Christ.

THE SONS OF KORAH

Throughout the many psalms David authored, speckled in are psalms that were written by the sons of Korah. The sons of Korah were the descendants of Kohath in the Old Testament; Kohath was a part of the tribe of Levi. In Numbers 4, the family of Kohath had a special part in covering and moving the most holy things of the Tabernacle when the children of Israel needed to journey. This was an honor and a high privilege that wasn't just allotted to anyone— they were ordained by God to do so.

Fast forwarding to chapter 16, Korah has a change of heart and ends up challenging Moses and Aaron's office. Korah and some others mustered up 250 men of Israel to confront them. Korah felt Moses and Aaron took too much upon themselves and exalted themselves over the rest of the assembly, as if they were holier. This is why it's important to guard our thoughts against the enemy, because he will try to plant seeds of discord among the body of Christ. The Bible says in 2 Corinthians 10:5 (NKJV), "…*bringing every thought into captivity to the obedience of Christ.*" We must cast down thoughts that are against our brothers and sisters in Christ Jesus, or anyone. So Korah formed a rebellion against Moses and Aaron, which in turn caused Moses to pray and come up with a solution. He said, "Tomorrow, let us all come out with censers full of incense and stand before the Lord, and we will see who belongs to Him and who He has chosen." The next day they were all assembled before the tabernacle with the censers. God told Moses and the congregation to move away from Korah, Dathan, Abiram, and their families. The earth opened up and swallowed these three rebellious men, along with their families. The rest of the 250 men with their censers ran, fearing they would be swallowed alive. As they ran, fire came out from the Lord and consumed them all. This was a grim ending for Korah and his followers, because they had challenged God Himself.

Even though God destroyed most of Korah's family, we find in Numbers 26:9-11 (NKJV) that his children, along with Dathan's and Abiram's, were not all consumed; it could well be that they were babies at the time of God's judgment and were spared. It says, *The sons of Eliab were Nemuel, Dathan, and Abiram. These are the Dathan and Abiram, representatives of the congregation, who contended against Moses and Aaron in the company of Korah, when they contended against the Lord; and the earth opened its mouth and swallowed them up together with Korah when that company died, when the fire devoured two hundred and fifty men; and they became a sign.*

Nevertheless the children of Korah did not die." Through the generations they learned from the mistakes of their ancestors. They were able to overcome the stigma of what had happened in the past. The prophet Samuel descended from the Kohathites, and his grandson Heman was a singer whom David appointed to minister before the Tabernacle, along with other musicians, in 1 Chronicles 6:22-38. They were also gatekeepers in the Tabernacle and in charge of the work of the service; in 1 Chronicles 9:19 (NKJV), *"Shallum the son of Kore, the son of Ebiasaph, the son of Korah, and his brethren, from his father's house, the Kora- hites, were in charge of the work of the service, gatekeepers of the tabernacle. Their fathers had been keepers of the entrance to the camp of the Lord."* Korah's family was redeemed and restored to their proper positions. Romans 11:29 (NKJV) says, *"For the gifts and the calling of God are irrevocable."*

In conclusion, who said you were like your family's past mistakes? Who said you had to be like them? We see the descendants of Korah become men of God, who loved God with all their hearts and wrote beautiful psalms. Your future is different than your ancestors' and is a future to look forward to. Embrace what God has for you; you won't be disappointed.

CHAPTER 5

Created in Christ Jesus for Good Works

One of the biggest questions people ask is, why am I here? What is my purpose on the earth? After we've finished school, settled into our careers, and life hands us a routine, sometimes we are left with a feeling of, *Is this all there is?* Now I am not saying to be ungrateful—these are blessings—but it's not all there is. God has so much more for you and me. There are dreams and aspirations inside of all of us that keep us going forward each day. There are also processes the Lord is taking us through to form us, so He can take us to new levels of glory.

If you are one of those who don't know what your calling is in life, or you're serving in church but don't feel like you know what your ministry is, this verse will help. Ecclesiastes 9:10 (NKJV) says, *"Whatever your hand finds to do, do it with your might; for there is no work or device or knowledge or wisdom in the grave where you are going."* Serve wherever God has planted you, meaning that if they are feeding the homeless, go; if they are visiting the nursing home, go; if they are evangelizing outside, go—and live your everyday life with expectation. When Elijah's mantle was thrown onto Elisha in 1 Kings 19:19, he was working; it wasn't ministry work, but he was going about his daily life when his calling presented itself. Look at Moses in Exodus 3:1-3—he was tending his father-in-law's sheep when he saw the burning bush. When you are active in the things of the Lord, or just everyday life, He will guide you toward your destiny and the doors will start to open for you. I had attended the Assemblies of God Spanish Eastern District Bible Institute for four years. It was prophesied to me while I was there in the office that one day I would teach there. Five years after graduating, I was called to teach the first-year class for a semester. I didn't have to knock on any doors; it came to me. As you walk, God will put the flooring down and make a path for you. You may say, "Five years—that's a long time," but in the interim I was working and serving at my church, helping out whenever I could. So, while you might be at a job or in a position that you're not happy about, do your best there, and work as if you're working for the Lord. It says in Colossians 3:23-24 (NKJV), *"And whatever you do, do it heartily, as to the Lord and not to men, knowing that from the Lord you will receive the reward of the inheritance; for you serve the Lord Christ."* Also, when you are faithful in the little things, He is able to put bigger things into your hands.

"His lord said to him, 'Well done, good and faithful

servant; you have been faithful over a few things, I will make you ruler over many things. Enter into the joy of your lord.'"

Matthew 25:23 NKJV

DON'T GET IMPATIENT

Yes, God takes His time. I'm sure we all know this verse in the Bible: 2 Peter 3:8 (NKJV), *"But, beloved, do not forget this one thing, that with the Lord one day is as a thousand years, and a thousand years as one day."* Whatever you do, don't rush God—one mistake we can make is getting so impatient for the promises to come to pass that we end up going ahead of God, trying to make them happen. If God tells you wait, then wait; go, then go; no, then it's no; and yes, then it's yes. It takes patience and a sense of self-discipline to listen when the Lord speaks and to obey. Trust me, it's better to wait on the Lord than to do things your way, and it ends up taking twice as much time to get where God wants you. When we listen to Him, things might take longer than we expect, but we'll be in God's will and in His blessing.

God is working behind the scenes. There are things He is putting in order for you. If these things are not done, then you will not come across the right people, the right job, the right spouse, etc. There have been times when I was praying, asking Jesus about why something was taking so long, and that is exactly what He would tell me: "I am working and putting things in order." Trust that God knows what He is doing. He is working for your good, and when the time is right, you'll have what you've been waiting for.

THE APOSTLE PAUL

We can look at the Apostle Paul and see a man completely devoted to preaching the gospel wherever the Lord sent him. He went to places outside of Israel, took ships, and ended up in jail, beaten, and mocked. He was devoted to the faith and put it all on the line for the furtherance of the gospel of Jesus Christ. In Acts 9, Jesus called and blinded Paul while on the road to Damascus, where he had planned to persecute the church he would soon help to build. After receiving his sight, Paul did not automatically begin his ministry; it took a little over seventeen years to come to pass.

After Ananias prayed for Paul in verses 17-18, he was baptized and began preaching in the Jewish synagogues. After many days, the Jews planned to kill Paul, but he was able to escape by being lowered down the city wall in a large basket. Now this is where the timeline starts in Galatians 1 and 2—Paul goes from Damascus to Arabia, then back to Damascus for three years, then to Jerusalem to see Peter for fifteen days, then to Syria and Cilicia; he then speaks about the churches in Judea; then after four-

teen years he goes to Jerusalem by revelation and begins
his ministry preaching to the Gentiles. Not much is written
about what happened during those years, but I can imagine Paul was going through a process similar to ours. I'm
sure that whatever happened during those seventeen years
served as a foundation that Paul was able to stand on and
that would keep him afloat for the rest of his ministry. What
we learn in the process is so important and shouldn't be
rushed. If you are in an in-between season, soak up whatever you can, because it'll help you in the tomorrow. Paul was
able to live out his ministry until the end; it is believed that
Paul died a martyr in Rome.

CHAPTER 6

Beloved

You are God's beloved. Nothing can separate you from His love—no height nor depth, nor anything that can happen in life. He is closer than we think, attentive to all of our ways, and more interested in our lives than we can ever imagine. What we may think is little and unimportant, Jesus is very interested in.

He made us in His image and likeness, and so when He sees you, He sees an extension of Himself. The Father loves you just like He loves Jesus. He gave His all for us, and I want you to know how important you are to God. Let us take a look at the Song of Solomon, also known as the Song of Songs, in the Bible. Here is a love between a man and a woman that you would think only happened in the movies. They are both lovestruck and determined to be with one another. Scholars in the past have tried to spiritualize this book by comparing the bride and groom to Israel and God, then later Christ and the church. But I can tell you this: the love of God goes deeper than the love of any human being. He is faithful.

Unfortunately, marriages end over different things

like weight gain, age, unattraction, falling out of love, etc. Times change and the years go by, but a commitment at the marriage altar should always be honored. It's important to maintain your love for one another and be aware when the enemy shows up to bring division. Our relationship with the Lord is the same—we have to pour our hearts into it so we don't get cold. It's important to have an everyday relationship with Jesus and spend one-on-one time with Him alone. He is the faithful Prince of Peace who adores His children and who would do absolutely anything just to be near them. No matter how many years go by—if our hair turns gray, if our appearance changes, whether a person loses a limb—the Lord doesn't change; He is still with us, embracing us. He is the lover of our souls, and just like the young man and woman in the Song of Songs, He is in love with His church.

There are parts of the Song of Songs where the young lady has a dream that she can't find her love, and she goes out into the streets to try and find him. Sometimes we will not feel the presence of God in our lives, but that doesn't mean He's not with us. We have to believe God at His word that He would never leave us or forsake us. He is always watching and attentive to our prayers, thoughts, and how we're feeling.

Jesus is your confidante, the One who won't turn His back on you; the Faithful One. Even when we have strayed,

He is still there, calling us back like He did Israel when they went after different lovers. Jesus remains the same, and His arms are open wide, calling us back home. He is ready to forgive our wanderings and ready to dress us in a clean, white robe of righteousness. Lean into Jesus and lay your burdens down; He is the faithful lover of our souls.

Until we meet Jesus and are together with Him in the sky, we are restricted to these earthly bodies. He has given us His Holy Spirit as a guarantee that He'll be back for us. In the meantime, keep your relationship with the Lord fruitful and of high priority, remembering that nothing can separate you from the love of God.

> *For I am persuaded that neither death nor life, nor angels nor principalities nor powers, nor things present nor things to come, nor height nor depth, nor any other created thing, shall be able to separate us from the love of God which is in Christ Jesus our Lord.*

Romans 8:38-39 (NKJV)

BEAUTY FOR ASHES

Today, if this book finds you sitting in ashes, I am glad to tell you that there is beauty awaiting you. People can look fine on the outside, but inside the soul could be sitting in ashes, mourning for something lost. It could be a broken relationship with God, a physical loss, or a sin issue. In the ancient Jewish customs, the Hebrews would put ashes on their head or literally sit in ashes when they mourned for the dead or were repenting. It's a sign of discomfort and a way of saying, "I'm not okay."

Today, if this is you, I want you to examine yourself and get to the root of why you're there. You can be open and honest with Jesus about your feelings, disappointments, or hurts. In the book of Isaiah, Israel had sinned against God; their hearts were far from Him, they were quick to shed blood, perverted justice, and did not defend the fatherless or the widow. They even sacrificed blemished, blind, and lame animals to God, which was prohibited in the Old Testament Law. Israel and Judah had gotten God to the point of no return. He was going to bring judgment upon them, and it came through a man named King Nebuchadnezzar. King Nebuchadnezzar took Israel and Judah into captivity and brought them to Babylon for seventy years. There, God told them to plant vineyards and build houses—in other words, get comfortable, because you'll be here awhile. The manner in which the Hebrews were taken captive was horrible. Many people were killed, and Solomon's beautiful temple was destroyed. The Hebrews were distraught to see what had become of their land, but it came as a consequence of disobedience.

Even though all this happened, God still had a plan for the nation. He would build them back up again, heal and bind their wounds, and give them a fresh start. As long as you're alive, you have the opportunity to start over again. Many of us have gone through a period of ruins in our lives where all seems lost, like a bad memory, and we are sitting in the ashes, but this is where Jesus comes in to lift up your head. There is not much that can be done about the past; it's gone and over with, but there is a present and a tomorrow awaiting your attention. It's possible for the ashes to come off and the carnage to be left behind. God told Israel in Isaiah 61, which I encourage you to read, "I will give you beauty for ashes." There is a tomorrow with your name on it—whether it's a breakthrough, new job, a spouse, a career, health—don't give up. It's possible to smile again and to walk into your destiny. You will not lose out on what God has for you, in Jesus' name!

The Spirit of the Lord God is upon Me, because the Lord has anointed Me to preach good tidings to the poor; He has sent Me to heal the brokenhearted, to proclaim liberty to the captives, and the opening of the prison to those who are bound; to proclaim the acceptable year of the Lord, and the day of vengeance of our God; to comfort all who mourn, to console those who mourn in Zion, to give them beauty for ashes, the oil of joy for mourning, the garment of praise for the spirit of heaviness; that they may be called trees of righteousness, the planting of the Lord, that He may be glorified.

Isaiah 61:1-3 (NKJV)

CHAPTER 7

Crucifying the Flesh

Crucifying the flesh is a pivotal point in our Christian walk. This is when we start to let go of our own will and desires and to agree with God and His will for our lives. It causes friction and it's displeasing to the flesh, because our ways are sometimes not God's ways for our lives. We can set out a map for our future—what school we want to attend, or the person we want to marry—but that may not be God's will. It's a process of totally emptying yourself of you and allowing Jesus to take full control. It's saying, "Okay God, despite what I want to do, despite what I want to say or how I want to react, I will choose to listen to You and take the godly route, even if it doesn't look like it's in my favor." Proverbs 3:5-6 (NKJV) says, *"Trust in the Lord with all your heart, and lean not on your own understanding; in all your ways acknowledge Him, and He shall direct your paths."* This verse is key to remember during the process. Remember, God just wants the best for you, and the flesh on its own will lead us outside of God's will. The Bible says in Proverbs 14:12 (NKJV), *"There is a way that seems right to a man, but its end is the way of death."*

So daily, as you're walking through life, situations will

present themselves that will give you a perfect opportunity to choose to align yourself with God's will and not your own. I'll give you an example: I was on a crowded train again in the Bronx on the downtown line, going to work. I was standing by one of the doors, looking outside, and before the doors closed a woman hit me with her whole body and pushed herself inside, and the doors closed; she then took an unapologetic stance and gave me a nasty look. Now there, I had a decision to make—either to go according to the flesh that says defend yourself, tell her off, in an extreme case push her back, or to move away from her and give it to God. Now I understand that this is not something that people will generally stay quiet about, and a reaction could come in less than a second, but remember—we have the Holy Spirit of God, and one of His fruits is self-control. For anyone, this could have sparked a major explosion of anger and things could have gotten disruptive, but we have to learn how to pick and choose our battles. So, I chose to move away and squeeze through some other people and say, "Jesus, I worship You," and when I said it, it did not come from a place of attitude. It was honest toward the Lord. Making decisions like that, even if you feel like you do want to say something but hold yourself for the sake of being obedient to God—right there you just crucified your flesh, and as situations continue to present themselves, you're going to find it easier to choose God's way until it becomes second nature.

I've seen people lose control and make fools out of themselves because of pride; people have lost jobs and even their lives because of this. Now I am not saying to never stick up for yourself, but you have to know when to hold back, because the enemy likes to bait us so we can get out of character. The battle is not between flesh and blood, like the apostle Paul says in Ephesians 6:10-18. We must put on the full armor of God and ask God to help us discern certain situations.

Galatians 5:16-26 gives us a breakdown of walking in the Spirit and the works of the flesh. God is well aware that there is a struggle in every human being to do what is right, and as Christians we have the Holy Spirit of God, who points us in the right direction. To walk in the Spirit simply means to obey the Spirit. In verses 16-17 (NKJV) it says, *"I say then: Walk in the Spirit, and you shall not fulfill the lust of the flesh. For the flesh lusts against the Spirit, and the Spirit against the flesh; and these are contrary to one another, so that you do not do the things that you wish."*

There is a tug-of-war over us, but we have the free will to make the right decisions. When you feed something, it grows—if you feed your spirit man more than the flesh, your spirit man will be strong and be able to overcome temptation. Feeding your spirit man consists of reading the Word, praying, and worshipping God; these things will strengthen your connection with God, and it'll cause you to want to be more like Him. The workings of the flesh are listed in verses 19-21 (NKJV): *"Now the works of the flesh are evident, which are: adultery, fornication, uncleanness, lewdness, idolatry, sorcery, hatred, contentions, jealousies, outbursts of wrath, selfish ambitions, dissensions, heresies, envy, murders, drunkenness, revelries, and the like; of which I tell you beforehand, just as I also told you in time past, that those who practice such things will not inherit the kingdom of God."* After reviewing these verses, if you find yourself struggling with any of these, present them to the Lord and be honest. Jesus is always ready to forgive. We cannot free ourselves, as much as we try; that's why we need Jesus and the infilling of the Holy Spirit. He sets the captives free, and He will be more than willing and overjoyed that we have chosen to come to Him to ask for help.

As you continue to crucify the flesh and walk in the Spirit, you will see the fruits of the Holy Spirit start to manifest themselves in your life. They are listed in verses 22-23 (NKJV): *"But the fruit of the Spirit is love, joy, peace, longsuffering (enduring injury, trouble, or provocation long and patiently), kindness, goodness, faithfulness, gentleness, self-control."* Once you start walking in the Spirit, you'll see that what may have upset you in the past will not have the same effect on you. Now you can respond with grace and patience. Crucifying the flesh is not overnight and requires practice—you might not always get it right, but the key is to keep trying and praying to God for strength, because you are not in this alone. Take every challenge as an invitation to go a step higher.

TAKE CONTROL

Take control of your emotions, or else your emotions will take control of you. Every day we can experience emotions, whether good, bad, happy, or sad. It's a God-given attribute that He's given to everyone, but we should know when to say, "Okay, I'm going to do what I know is right instead of do as I feel." As Christians, we should know how to manage our emotions and make the right choices if a tense situation arises, and not be led astray.

There are people who live captive to their emotions and live an unbalanced life, constantly making poor choices. If I woke up every morning tired and not wanting to go to work, and I didn't, I wouldn't have a job. Or people who have an "I do as I want, I do as I feel" attitude constantly end up in unnecessary confrontations, and even jail. As Christians, it's important to be aware of our emotions and identify whether they are influencing how we're living and reacting to others. If we are living from a place of hurt, envy, pain, etc., then we'll have to get to the root of what it is and ask God to heal us so we can live free and be life-giving to others.

Covering unhealthy emotions doesn't make the situation any better; sooner or later they'll come out at an unexpected time. Now I want to give a backdrop to the story of 2 Samuel 15-17, so I'll summarize 2 Samuel 11-12. When kings were supposed to go to battle, King David stayed home and the rest of the army went out to fight. One night, David got up from bed and walked on the roof of his house, and he saw a woman bathing. He inquired who she was, and it was told to him that she was Bathsheba, the wife of Uriah the Hittite, one of his mighty warriors. Knowing this, David sent messengers to bring Bathsheba to his house, where he slept with her. Afterward, she conceived and sent word to David. David, attempting to cover up what had happened, summoned Uriah twice, made him drunk, and tried to get him to go home to lay with Bathsheba. Uriah, being a righteous man, would not go, because Israel was in a battle season. He slept at the door of the king's house, along with the rest of the men of Israel. David became desperate and sent a letter in the hand of Uriah to Joab, the commander of the army, to have Uriah positioned where the hottest battle would be so that he could be killed at war. Uriah, being the righteous man that he was, never opened the letter David sent by his hand to Joab which sealed his fate. Unfortunately, the plan worked, and Uriah died in battle. After Bathsheba had mourned her husband, David married her, but the child that was born to them died of sickness because the Lord was displeased with what David had done. David repented and God forgave him; later, David and Bathsheba would be the parents of King Solomon.

Now let's go to 2 Samuel 15-17. Ahithophel was King David's advisor, who sided easily with Absalom when he rebelled against David, his father. Absalom conspired against David, as we spoke of in an earlier chapter, and tried to overtake the kingdom. Instead of Ahithophel objecting to this and defending David, he went along with the conspiracy and even offered to ambush and kill David himself. According to 2 Samuel 23:34, Ahithophel had a son named Eliam, and in 2 Samuel 11:3 it says that Bathsheba was the daughter of Eliam, making Ahithophel Bathsheba's grandfather. It was a tight-knit community among the Israelites, and betrayal usually came from someone within an inner circle. Ahithophel hid his true emotions toward David, but they were revealed during Absalom's rebellion. Ahithophel might have greatly loved Uriah, Bathsheba's husband, and to witness how King David had betrayed Uriah and had his life taken in battle may have left him bitter.

The Bible says in 2 Samuel 16:23 (NKJV), *"Now the advice of Ahithophel, which he gave in those days, was as if one had inquired at the oracle of God. So was all the advice of Ahithophel both with David and with Absalom."* So, David sent Hushai the Archite, who was his companion, to defeat any counsel Ahithophel had given Absalom, and with God's help Hushai prevailed. When Ahithophel saw that his advice was rejected, he took his own life. Ahithophel's secret dislike for David led him down a slippery slope that didn't end well. Hebrews 4:13 (NKJV) says, *"And there is no creature hidden from His sight, but all things are naked and open to the eyes of Him to whom we must give account."*

Ahithophel's heart grew a root of bitterness, and he hid it well during his years with David. What would have freed him was confessing his feelings to God and to David. Considering David's character, I'm sure he would have apologized, and they could have mended their relationship. Ahithophel then could have stayed, or he could have left the king's house and gone his way. Sometimes, doing what we know is right over what we feel can bring a situation to light, and we can ask the Lord for healing and live life from a place of freedom.

But what if you bring up an offense to a person who caused you hurt and they deny you an apology? The best thing to do is to go into the presence of the Lord Jesus, and let Him deal with your wound and let Him heal you. Sometimes people will not own up to the hurt they have caused you, or they simply just don't care. That doesn't mean you have to live your life waiting for an apology that will never come. There is always a new horizon, and it's yours for the taking; you can either live bitter or live better. Learn from the situation, forgive, and move forward. Don't let anyone stifle your joy or the amazing future that God has for you through Christ Jesus. Keep pushing on, and you will see the glory of God in your life; leave the other person in God's hands.

Now after you've forgiven, it doesn't mean it's erased from your memory. If the old feelings try to come back and reopen that wound, rebuke it in Jesus' name and put your focus on Jesus. Read scripture, start to worship, put some music on and remember the faithfulness of our God, who got you through it. Guard your heart and guard your mind, and you'll be fine.

> *You will keep him in perfect peace, whose mind is stayed on You, because he trusts in You.*

> **Isaiah 26:3 (NKJV)**

THE HOLY SPIRIT

Jesus said in John 14:16-18 (KJV), *"And I will pray the Father, and he shall give you another Comforter, that he may abide with you for ever; even the Spirit of truth; whom the world cannot receive, because it seeth him not, neither knoweth him: but ye know him; for he dwelleth with you, and shall be in you. I will not leave you comfortless: I will come to you."*

You are not alone. God has sent His precious Holy Spirit to live inside of you. You are not just anyone—you have God's resurrection power living inside of you. He is your best friend, whom you can talk to regardless of the hour. He is there to empower you to live a God-fearing life and to convict you of any sin. He is the compass that will lead you into all holiness, and He also is your authority.

I encourage you to invoke the Holy Spirit's presence in your life. For example, before I leave my house and drive, I always pray and say, "Holy Spirit, you are in control; you drive the car," and there is always a peace that goes with me. I remember someone from church got into my car, and we were at a red light and she looked over at me and said, "There is such a peace in this car—wow." The presence of the Lord shows up wherever He is invited. Welcome Him into your home, job, any appointments you may have, and He will be right there with you. You might be saying, "But God is everywhere—what do you mean, welcome Him?" Sometimes we can treat the Holy Spirit like a guest that we never speak to—we are sealed by the Holy Spirit after we receive Christ and then have no further communication with Him. But when you engage the Holy Spirit and speak to Him, it makes all the difference, and the atmosphere will change.

Also, pray for the baptism of the Holy Spirit. This is such an important part of a believer's life. This is our empowerment. When we see that the disciples in the book of Acts 2 became empowered with the Holy Spirit, there was a boldness that came over them—especially Peter, who preached a sermon right on the spot, and three thousand souls were saved. The Holy Spirit is our lifeline, the Spirit of Jesus Christ. With God's power on your side and within you, you will not lose! You have access to the most powerful Spirit; commune with Him, ask Him for help when reading the scriptures, and He will enlighten you. You have a faithful Friend who will never fail you. He will lead you into all truth, comfort you in your distresses, and remind you of what the Word of God says. In the past, God's presence resided in the Most Holy Place in the Tabernacle on the ark of the covenant; you are now the holder of God's presence on the earth. Drink from the well that lives inside of you, and your soul will never be thirsty again.

In the last day, that great day of the feast, Jesus stood and cried, saying, If any man thirst, let him come unto me, and drink. He that believeth on me, as the scripture hath said, out of his belly shall flow rivers of living water. (But this spake he of the Spirit, which they that believe on him should receive: for the Holy Ghost was not yet given; because that Jesus was not yet glorified.)

John 7:37-39 (KJV)

CHAPTER 8

More Than a Conqueror

God did not merely design us to live life just "making it through." We were made to be overcomes, trailblazers, inventors, and so much more. God has set a standard for our lives, and it's excellence. Gideon, in the Bible, didn't think much of himself. He lived at a time in Israel when they had been oppressed by the Midianites for seven years. God permitted this, because Israel had done evil in His sight. When they planted crops, the Midianites, Amalekites, and people from the East would come and destroy their produce, forcing Israel into caves and strongholds in the mountains. The children of Israel were greatly impoverished and cried out to the Lord.

In Judges 6, the angel of the Lord appears to Gideon while he secretly threshes wheat by a winepress and says to him, "The Lord is with you, you mighty man of valor!" That is heaven's perspective of us, here on the earth. God made strong people—and how much more, being anointed and called by Him? Now Gideon didn't believe what the angel said about him, and verse 15 (NKJV) says, *"So he said to Him, 'O my Lord, how can I save Israel? Indeed my clan is the weakest in Manasseh, and I am the least in my father's house.'"* Like Gideon, sometimes we can look at ourselves as weak, and not enough, and think, *What difference can I make?* But one thing I've learned is that when you put yourself in God's hands and unite with His will, the impossible has to shatter. The self-perception has to change, and you'll see yourself as God sees you.

Fast forward to chapter 7—God separated 300 men to help Gideon overtake the armies of the Midianites, Amalekites, and the people of the East. These armies were asleep, encamped in a valley, and they looked like grasshoppers for multitude; it even says their camels were without number as the sand of the sea. Gideon was a little afraid, but God had guaranteed him the victory. At the request of Gideon, the men of Israel broke up into three groups of 100 and surrounded the camp. He instructed them that when he blew the trumpet, every man would blow theirs and break the pitchers they were carrying, and yell, "The sword of the Lord, and of Gideon!" When this happened, it caused major confusion in the enemies' camp—and they woke up and started attacking one another, and some ran for their lives. Gideon then sent word to some of the other tribes of Israel, and they came and pursed their enemies. The men of Ephraim seized the waters of Beth Barah and Jordan. There they captured two of the princes of the Midianites, Oreb and Zeeb, and brought their heads back to Gideon on the other side of the Jordan. That day, with the help of God,

Israel conquered their enemies.

Even though Gideon didn't believe in himself, God gave him the courage to go forward and fight. There is a warrior inside each of us, and sometimes we don't know it's there until we're put in a hard place. The struggles we go through in life will awaken that warrior. You are an overcomer; don't bend when the pressure comes, but walk in faith, knowing that the God of the universe, Jesus Christ, lives inside of you!

> *You are of God, little children, and have overcome them, because He who is in you is greater than he who is in the world.*

1 John 4:4 (NKJV)

DON'T FORGET WHO YOU ARE

I watch an eagle's nest in California, and it's so exciting when new baby eagles are born. They remain in the nest until they grow their adult feathers and then take flight. It dawned on me one day that these birds only know what type of animal they are by seeing their parents. They don't have a mirror and are elevated pretty high above other animals. When they fly away, they rarely see a reflection of themselves unless they are by water, but yet they know who they are. For example, you've never seen an eagle and an owl nesting together. The eagles stick to other eagles. If they know who they are, then we ought to know who we are.

Our identity is in Christ Jesus, and when we read the Word of God it reveals to us who we're truly designed to be: holy, righteous children of the Most High God. The world will try to strip us of this truth through deception and sin, but I want you to understand the true gem you are in Christ Jesus. The Bible says in James 1:22-25 (NKJV), *"But be doers of the word, and not hearers only, deceiving yourselves. For if anyone is a hearer of the word and not a doer, he is like a man observing his natural face in a mirror; for he observes himself, goes away, and immediately forgets what kind of man he was. But he who looks into the perfect law of liberty and continues in it, and is not a forgetful hearer but a doer of the work, this one will be blessed in what he does."* So, going forward, when you read or hear the Word of God, I want you to live it out. If you've been set free, live a life that expresses that; if you know you are valuable, don't settle for someone who will treat you as "less than." If you know you are loved, share that love with others. Be a doer of the Word in your life, not only a hearer, and apply it to your every day.

God bless you!

Salvation Prayer

Lord Jesus, I come before Your presence, believing that You are the Son of God. I accept You into my heart as my Lord and Savior and ask You to forgive me of all my sins.

Holy Spirit, I open my heart to You; make
Your home in me.

In Jesus' name,

amen.

~

My prayer for you is that the Holy Spirit will cover you, dwell in you, and guide you, all the days of your life!

References

1. King James Bible

2. New King James Bible

3. Complete Jewish Bible

4. Livestrong website:

   https://www.livestrong.com/article/533248-what-happen-to-your-muscles-when-you-work-out/

5. Got Questions:

   https://www.gotquestions.org/sons-of-Korah.html

6. Merriam-Webster.com